PR Proverbs

Your Launch Pad for an Exceptional Personal
and Professional Reputation

Glynnis Woolridge

Salt & Light Publishing

Salt & Light Publishing
Salt & Light Enterprises, LLC
3824 Cedar Springs Rd., Suite 139
Dallas, TX 75219

First Edition: May 2022

Salt & Light Publishing is a division of Salt & Light Enterprises, LLC. The Salt & Light Publishing name and logo are trademarks of Salt & Light Enterprises, LLC.

The publisher is not responsible for websites (or their content) that are not owned by the publisher.

All Scripture quotations, unless otherwise indicated, are taken from the Holy Bible, New International Version®, NIV®. Copyright ©1973, 1978, 1984, 2011 by Biblica, Inc.™ Used by permission of Zondervan. All rights reserved worldwide. www.zondervan.com. The "NIV" and "New International Version" are trademarks registered in the United States Patent and Trademark Office by Biblica, Inc.™

ISBN: 979-8-9856315-0-0 (paper back), 979-8-9856315-1-7 (ebook)

Printed in the United States of America

To my family, immediate and extended. Thank you for your prayers, words of encouragement and the enthusiasm with which you embarked upon this journey with me. I love you all.

CONTENTS

PART IV
Chill Down

PART V
Fuel Up

PART VI
Pre-Flight Calibration

PART VII
Launch Sequence Is A Go

PR Proverbs

Your Launch Pad for an Exceptional Personal
and Professional Reputation

PART I

ACTIVATE NAVIGATIONAL SYSTEMS

INTRODUCTION

Wisdom is supreme; therefore, get wisdom.
Though it cost you all you have, get understanding.

— Proverbs 4:7

It's a favorite question of interviewers: "If you could talk to your younger self, what advice would you give?" Gaining wisdom through life's many trials and triumphs is one of the benefits of growing older. Wouldn't you rather skip the wait and forego the mistakes?

Wisdom isn't always tied to age or experience. I've met teenagers who are wiser than some adults I know. Wisdom comes from God, the inventor of wisdom who gives it generously to all who ask (James 1:5). Have you put in your request?

The Bible characterizes wisdom as more precious than gold, silver or precious gems. It's no surprise, then, that the Book of Proverbs contains guidance on just about anything you can think of.

Want to know if you should take a nap after that big meal or work on your passion project that will bring you closer to financial freedom? *A little sleep, a little slumber, a little folding of the hands to rest – and poverty will come on you like a bandit and scarcity like an armed man* (6:10-11). Thinking about buying that exclusive club membership you can't afford just to be seen in the 'right circles'? *Better to be a nobody and yet have a servant than pretend to be somebody and have no food* (12:9). Wondering why someone who usually works against you at every turn is now working on your behalf? *When a man's ways are pleasing to the Lord, He makes even his enemies live at peace with him* (16:7). See?

The Book of Proverbs contains wisdom for your personal life, but the guidance and answers within its 31 chapters are just as relevant to your professional endeavors.

PR Proverbs translates the personal character lessons found in the Book of Proverbs into practical and actionable guidance that helps you build relationships and trust with your key audiences.

You may not have in-house expertise or the resources to hire an experienced public relations professional. You may have struggled through trial and error, learning the hard way how a seemingly simple statement or action (or lack thereof) can have a lasting effect on your reputation. If so, your journey to an exceptional reputation through a better understanding public relations begins now.

I've been blessed to work with some amazing public relations professionals during my career at local grassroots organizations as well as corporations that span industries and continents. PR Proverbs is born out of that experience.

Some of my own trials and observations make appearances in this book; there were plenty of times in my career where I didn't follow the PR Proverbs I'm sharing. I paid the price but learned valuable lessons. Spoiler alert: I'm still a work in progress!

Use this book as a guide to help you be wise in how you listen to, understand and build relationships with your audiences. Public relations is not about spinning a story or manipulating circumstances, although some have done that under the banner of the craft. The lifeblood of public relations is truth, integrity and trust.

Whether you're engaged in public relations for your personal brand or for a global company, the state of your reputation will determine your level of success.

Did you know that people are more likely to follow your leadership if they trust you, and that you are more likely to win that contract if your great reputation precedes you?

People are more likely to buy from you if your brand has a positive reputation. The vast majority (87%) of consumers around the world say that they take the reputation of the company into account when purchasing a product or service (https://www.ipsos.com/en/how-reputation-and-trust-affect-purchase-decisions-and-marketing-efficiency#:~:text=Building%20a%20good%20reputation%20generates,on%20what%20you're%20told).

This fact is not lost on C-Suite leadership who are paying attention: a survey of global executives found that they attribute 63% of their company's value to its reputation (https://www.webershandwick.com/news/corporate-reputation-2020-everything-matters-now/).Think about that for a moment. A good reputation accounts for more than half of a company's value. What are you potentially missing out on because your reputation is not living up to its full potential?

If your public relations efforts are falling flat, the strategy you toiled over is not accomplishing what you need it to, or if you just can't seem to change the perception people have about your product or service, then perhaps it's time to look beyond the "function" of public relations and inspect the "foundation" it is resting on. It may have some cracks. Everyone knows that if a foundation is cracked, the entire structure is in danger.

Attaining and maintaining anything of value requires diligence, dedication and time. There are no easy fixes or shortcuts. Likewise, an exceptional brand reputation is built, not bought. You have to work at it continuously. Take the wisdom of PR Proverbs and put it into action, every day.

The one who gets wisdom loves life; the one who cherishes understanding will soon prosper.

—Proverbs 19:8

Here's to wisdom, love and prosperity in all areas of your life.

PUBLIC RELATIONS: WHAT IT IS/ISN'T

*Listen to advice and accept discipline, and at
the end you will be counted among the wise.*

—Proverbs 19:20

I used to get annoyed when I heard people say, "Anyone can
do PR; all you have to do is talk to people." Or, "I think I'll
go into public relations because I'm a people person!"

My public relations colleagues and I would snort. We
studied for years in school, earned our degrees in public
relations, communications and journalism, and honed our
skills in the most challenging corporate environments. What
do you mean, "anyone can do it?"

Truth be told, when it comes to your reputation, you're
a public relations practitioner whether you realize it or not.
Being concerned with your character, reputation and brand is
not limited to the realm of business. These things spring from
our personal beliefs and behavior, and we bring our personal
to the professional.

It can be difficult to settle on a succinct definition
of public relations because it is the foundation of many
other disciplines, including Social Media, Marketing

Communications, Content Creation, Integrated Marketing, Brand Management, Community Relations, Employee Communications, Media Relations, Crisis Communications, Investor Relations Communications, Events, Speech writing and, of course, Reputation Management.

Public relations is not a way to 'spin a story' or a constant dribble of press releases. Public relations efforts are not spectacles that mask tricks and sleight-of-hand. It's much more than hounding a reporter to cover your news, and it's definitely not shaking hands and kissing babies.

Public relations is about understanding, engaging and building relationships with key stakeholders across numerous platforms in order to shape and frame the public perception of an organization (https://www.prsa.org/about/all-about-pr).

Whether you're building a business or brand, wading through a crisis, fighting for visibility in a competitive market or championing a worthy cause, a credible public relations effort is key to your success.

To be effective in your quest to create a positive perception, you must understand the interdependencies of your words, actions, reputation and the perception your key audiences hold of you. These things are inextricably linked.

Here's the good news: you don't have to be an experienced public relations professional to understand and apply the basic principles of public relations to your situation. It's true that a good portion of public relations savvy comes from education and experience, but just as much is born out of wisdom and plain old common sense.

Every culture has proverbs. Some are unique and some are shared in one form or another among all cultures. Proverbs are not just witty sayings but are nuggets of wisdom and practical advice applicable to just about any situation. There is no better place to get wisdom than the Bible, the Book of Proverbs in particular.

So, if public relations and reputation management seem a bit daunting, you're in the right place. PR Proverbs: Your Launch Pad for an Exceptional Personal and Professional Reputation will demystify basic aspects of public relations and help you be the best expression of yourself.

Like the book of the Bible that is its namesake, every PR Proverb is its own gem of public relations wisdom related to your character: the values that govern who you are, what you say and what you do.

PR Proverbs provides a guide to help you establish a solid foundation on which to build an exceptional reputation. It's not a "how to" book that explains the fundamental elements of a press release, 10 ways to get an article placement or the best social media platform to use. Tactics change and delivery mechanisms come and go. Your character and reputation, however, last your lifetime and beyond. It's time to take hold of the steering wheel because the vehicle is already in motion (and has been for quite some time).

Whether you're an entrepreneur, community leader or CEO of a brand known around the world, the wisdom of PR Proverbs will enlighten and elevate your approach to engaging with your key publics.

With truth and honesty at your core, wisdom as your mantle, and a willingness to listen and learn, you can build and maintain an invaluable asset - an excellent reputation. Are you ready?

PR Proverbs

Your Launch Pad for an Exceptional Personal
and Professional Reputation

Proverbs 1

1 The proverbs of Solomon son of David, king of Israel:

2 for gaining wisdom and instruction;
for understanding words of insight;

3 for receiving instruction in prudent behavior,
doing what is right and just and fair;

4 for giving prudence to those who are simple,
knowledge and discretion to the young—

5 let the wise listen and add to their learning,
and let the discerning get guidance—

6 for understanding proverbs and parables,
the sayings and riddles of the wise.

7 The fear of the LORD is the beginning of knowledge,
but fools despise wisdom and instruction.

PART II

PREPARE FOR LAUNCH

START HERE

Trust in the Lord with all your heart and lean not on your own understanding. In all your ways acknowledge Him, and He will make your paths straight.

—Proverbs 3:5-6

You may be tempted to jump right to the part about what *you* want to say, what *you* want to communicate, the messages *you* need to get out there or the article *you* want published. Do you see a pattern here? You are important, but you're not the starting point.

Here's where to start: *If any of you lacks wisdom, you should ask God, who gives generously to all without finding fault, and it will be given to you* (James 1:5). It all begins with the Giver of wisdom.

Why does all this wisdom stuff matter? It matters because public relations isn't an exact science. Success or failure often rests on choices and judgment calls, many times without the luxury of a lot of time to think about it.

Consider this scenario: A clothing company executive just learned about the passing of a well-loved celebrity who happened to be a fan of the company's product. Millions around the world are discussing the life and legacy of this person, voraciously reading and watching everything about the celebrity.

The executive immediately recalls a picture of that celebrity wearing a product that has underperformed against this year's sales targets. The salesperson inside the executive's mind thinks, *this is a great opportunity! I'll post that picture, express condolences and put a link to the product in the comments. Millions of people will see and want to buy the product - sales will climb through the roof!*

Hopefully, the proverbial public relations person inside *your* mind recoiled as you read that scenario. Bad idea, right? Opportunistic and insensitive, right? Then why does this type of hypothetical scenario continue to play out in reality despite the negative backlash it unleashes?

It's because we typically lean to our own understanding instead of relying on God's direction and wisdom. I'm not minimizing the skills you or I have, but our natural inclinations are not always best. You'll be better prepared for the next "opportunity" if you acknowledge God and ask for His wisdom and understanding.

I'm not professing that every decision you make will be the perfect one, but the more you base your decision-making on the wisdom you ask God for, the more you will start to see those requests bear fruit.

The more you ask for and apply wisdom, the easier it will become to step outside of your own thoughts and see situations from a 360-degree vantage point. Trust God to reveal things you may be missing or misunderstanding. If you're humble enough to ask God daily for His wisdom, you will be amazed at what you will learn and be able to discern.

Don't wait for a precarious situation to arise before you start praying for wisdom. Seeking God's guidance - on big decisions, small choices and everything in between - will deliver dividends that will flow out of you when you need it most.

THE HEART OF THE MATTER

*Above all else, guard your heart, for
everything you do flows from it.*

—Proverbs 4:23

Far too often, this scenario unfolds: a person says or writes something inappropriate, crass or downright hateful, then issues an apology stating, "that's not who I really am." Yes, it is.

What comes out of your mouth originates from what has been living inside your heart. Perhaps it was something you were taught as a child. It could be the result of something you spend too much time watching or reading. Maybe you are influenced by the company you keep. Whatever the case, what's on the inside will eventually come out – and at the most inopportune moment!

There is a saying that inside every individual are six people:
1. Who you are reputed to be
2. Who you are expected to be
3. Who you were
4. Who you wish to be
5. Who you think you are
6. Who you really are

You may work hard to show the world a version of yourself that is in line with what you feel the public wants to see, but who you really are will win out every single time. Who you really are flows out of your heart.

If inclusion is a core value of the company you lead but you personally don't value inclusion, it's going to show in your hiring practices and in the composite of your staff - from senior leaders to new hires. If you profess to love and accept all people and yet treat them differently based on how they look, dress or worship, your mouth and heart are out of alignment.

Public relations can be challenging work. It becomes nearly impossible when your desired reputation is at odds with your words and actions. As you align who you are reputed to be, who you wish to be and who you really are, your reputation will soon begin to rise to the level of excellence you need for an exceptional reputation.

Be honest with yourself and come to grips with who you really are. While the previous chapter dealt primarily with what you say and do, this assessment peers into your values and beliefs - the core of who you are.

We all have things we need to work on and work through, so take a deep look inward. You may discover things about yourself - biases, assumptions, etc. - that are preventing you from the reputation breakthrough you desire.

Start by focusing on one thing. Taking on everything at once may be a tall order. It takes a while to reprogram behavior, about 10 weeks according to studies (https://www.ncbi.nlm.nih.gov/pmc/articles/PMC3505409/). Some attitudes take much longer to change.

I used to work at a global payment card company. My manager recommended me for the organization's leadership training program that puts participants on a fast track to senior-level positions. Each year, a small cohort was selected to participate in this weeks-long curriculum focused on global business strategy, financial operations, corporate governance, sales and marketing, leadership skills, product development, negotiation and other topics.

At the end of the program, a capstone project was given to the cohort in the form of a business pitch for a new financial services product. We were placed in teams and given a deadline for completing the group project. We all had come to know each other, given the cohort size, and I was excited about the group I landed in. We all had different strengths but seemed to have a like-minded approach to the project. Well...almost all of us.

There was one young man who was always off to the side and would never participate in the conversation. The discussions were lively and fast-paced; every other member of the team jumped in at one point or another with input. He never did.

Typical, I thought. *There's always one person who sits back and lets everyone else do the heavy lifting but shows up at the end to reap the rewards.*

As we worked through each phase of the project, we grew more annoyed at his lack of participation. Eventually, we ignored him and rolled forward with the project. Time was running out, and we had a competition to win.

The executive mentors called an end to the planning session and lined up "Shark Tank" style to hear the pitches.

Given the pitches presented before ours, we knew we had this in the bag. Our time came, and we nailed it! Or, so we thought. One element of our proposal had a major flaw that we didn't notice in our haste to get the presentation done before time ran out. The executives started poking holes in our proposal and things began to crumble.

That's when the young man who never opened his mouth began to speak. He identified the issue and described a solution that blew away the executives. They turned to the rest of us and asked, "Why didn't you present his idea?" We stood silent and dumbfounded.

After the exercise was over (we didn't win), we turned to go back to our original places scattered throughout the room. Before walking away, I turned to the young man and asked, "If you knew there was a gaping hole in our strategy, why didn't you say something earlier?" He looked up and in a quiet voice said, "You never asked."

A retort was on the tip of my tongue when he continued. "I'm kind of an introvert, I guess. It takes me a while to feel comfortable in this type of environment. I like to take my time thinking things through. By the time I figured it out, you all had made up your minds about what to present. I didn't think you wanted to hear what I had to say."

He walked away, and I was left standing there speechless and dumbfounded for the second time in less than five minutes.

Why was I so quick to assume that the young man's silence was because he was disinterested or ill-equipped for the challenge? Because that's what was in my heart. I was quick to judge people who acted differently than how I thought they should.

Once I acknowledged that, I remembered other times when I did the same thing. That was not a good feeling, let me tell you. Right then, I decided to make changes in my thought process and behavior. Trust me, changing that behavior took longer than 10 weeks!

I'm airing one of my shortcomings with the hope that it will make you more comfortable in addressing yours. Don't pass off what you wrote or said as a one-off or something you did in the heat of the moment. No one really believes that anyway.

Check your heart, own your behavior and resolve to be a person of good character.

HOW DO PEOPLE SPELL YOUR NAME?

A good name is more desirable than great riches;
to be esteemed is better than silver or gold.

— Proverbs 22:1

U-n-r-e-l-i-a-b-l-e? D-i-s-h-o-n-e-s-t?

The mere mention or thought of your name immediately conjures up a perception of your image, character and reputation in someone's mind. It doesn't matter whether or not the person actually *knows* you. What comes to mind when they *think* of you?

You live in parallel universes: the world of Reality (who you are), and the world of Perception (who people think you are and what they think about you).

Perceptions and opinions begin to form long before a person encounters you or your business. What they have learned indirectly about you from word-of-mouth, your website, or something they read or watched led to an assumption about you?

That assumption - the perception people have of you, your company, products or services - is the Goliath you have to fight if there is a disparity between who you are and how people see you. There are ways to defeat your Goliath and change perceptions. We'll get into that a little later in this chapter.

Direct encounters set immediate and lasting perceptions. It's tough to change someone's mind when they have personal experience with an individual or product. What type of experiences have people had with you? Hopefully, your encounters with them reinforce your "good name."

A few friends of mine loved to pull pranks back in high school. Once, I was lured into being an unwitting accomplice for a prank on our cheerleading coach. My friends' intent was to do the deed and have all the evidence point toward me.

By the time I caught on to what they were up to, it was too late. The prank went south, we got busted and were called into the coach's office. At the end of the conversation, I walked out unscathed and my friends didn't.

Want to know why? My reputation preceded me. After my friends presented their case that pointed in my direction, our cheerleading coach uttered the nickname that would stay with me for the rest of my high school journey: "Not 'Good-As-Gold Glynnis'. She would never do something like that!"

That's the power of a good name. My words, actions and encounters with our cheerleading coach had built up a positive reputation with her that stood against an accusation that I was the mastermind of the prank.

Well, not that particular prank, anyway. My realization of what a positive reputation could do caused me to push the envelope a time or two before I graduated (don't judge). Thankfully, smart phones weren't around back then, so there's no evidence to besmirch my nickname.

Your name or reputation may not be "good-as-gold" right now. What do you do? Gather some stones and get ready to take down Goliath.

Start by taking a good look in the mirror. Be objective and evaluate why the perception is the way it is. It could be due to a misunderstanding or because of misinformation. Many times, if we're honest, it's because we've done something (or failed to do something we should have done) that contributed to a poor reputation.

If you're brave enough, ask a family member, a trusted friend or a mentor to give you an honest opinion about your character. Create a safe zone for them to speak bluntly. You may be shocked to learn how they perceive you, but don't take offense! Truth from a friend is better than flattery from an enemy pretending to be a friend (*Wounds from a friend can be trusted, but an enemy multiplies kisses.* Proverbs 27:6).

Do they think you are honest? Do you trust you? How do you come across when you're communicating with people? Are you a person of your word? The answers to these types of questions will give you an indication of the condition of your reputational foundation.

Now that you have constructive feedback, it's time to evaluate and plan a course of action. Think about the feedback in two ways: what perception(s) did you earn, and what perception(s) did you enable?

An earned perception is a result of what you consciously say or don't say and what you consciously do or don't do. Your conscious decisions - good, bad or indifferent - contribute to the way people perceive you. Know it and own it.

On the flip side, perceptions you enable are those that result from actions you are not conscious of but they leave an impression just the same.

Do you have an unconscious habit of tapping a pen or pencil on the conference table during meetings? You may come across as rude to the person who's presenting a report that took weeks to prepare. With each tap, you are enabling the perception of you being a disruptive co-worker who is dismissive of others' hard work.

Whether you're earning or enabling, it's time to pay closer attention to how your actions are perceived by others. With an open heart and a willing mind, acknowledge and change behaviors that are detrimental to how you want to be perceived. Invest in those that reinforce the reputation you want to have.

Be consistent. Line up your behavior with who you say you are, and the perception will slowly come around to the reality.

PART III

CLEAR THE BLAST DANGER AREA

DID I JUST SAY THAT?

Even fools are thought wise if they keep silent,
and discerning if they hold their tongues.

—Proverbs 17:28

The following quote is attributed to several people and has been circulating in one form or another since the mid-1900s: *"We all know that light travels faster than sound. That's why certain people appear bright until you hear them speak."* I'm convinced that Proverbs 17:28, circa 700 BC, is its origin.

No one knows everything about anything. There will always be things we simply don't know or understand. When you find yourself in a new environment or in a situation where you don't normally operate, just listen. A voice inside your head may scream, *say something so people will know how smart you are!*, but don't be in such a rush to speak. Get comfortable with silence. There is power in just being in the room.

Soak up every word, every nuance, every movement. You will be amazed at what you learn - and what you notice - when you're humble enough to not talk when it isn't necessary to speak.

If a point has already been made, resist the urge to repeat it by using different words and phrases. Choose instead to expand or build on the idea, or make a connection between the current point and a different (but related) idea that others may have missed. It is better to follow up after the meeting with a powerful observation or idea than to blurt out something stupid in the moment.

Let me say this before you think I'm telling you to sit down and shut up: I'm not advocating that you should never speak up, just make your voice heard when you have something of substance to say. Especially if you have not yet grasped the art of listening.

There have been countless research studies and opinion pieces on active listening - what it is, how to do it, and the parts of the brain that are engaged in the process. I have a much simpler method for minimizing the disconnects between your ears and mouth. There are four simple steps: hear, listen, understand, speak.

Hearing. Have you ever been so engrossed in something that you didn't hear someone calling your name? Be present in the moment and engaged in what's going on so you can hear. You can daydream or figure out what's for dinner later. This first step is not just relevant to conversation; if your perceptual ears are fine-tuned, you can also "hear" the sound of change, opportunity and trouble approaching. This first step can help you stay ahead of the game. Be observant.

Listening. Hearing is the sound, listening is the content. Pay attention and absorb what is being said. Truly listen instead of spending that time formulating your next statement. Everyone's voice is important and needs to be heard. You may not agree with every point of view, but your perspective will be enriched. Keep the interruptions to a minimum unless you need clarification on what is being said.

Understanding. Repeating back words or sentences does not mean you understand what someone told you. Understanding is not just knowing *what* a person said, but *why*. Knowing why illuminates the real reason for the statement or point of view. It's much easier to find common ground or solve a problem when you understand the motivation behind what a person is communicating. Heads up: your behavior may be at the heart of someone else's why, and you may need to adjust your behavior to make things right.

Speaking. Now that you heard, listened and understood, you are well-equipped to speak from a position of knowledge and confidence. You haven't jumped to conclusions or failed to see things from different perspectives. Get right to the point, sharing your insight and weaving in others' input to show they have been heard and understood. When people feel included, they are more likely to align with a common goal.

As you get more astute at listening to others, you'll find that when it's your turn to speak, your words will hold more power. You will have proved that when you speak, you have something of value to offer. You won't just appear to be wise, you will be.

THE MIC IS ALWAYS ON

Those who guard their lips preserve their lives,
but those who speak rashly will come to ruin.

—**Proverbs 13:3**

The term "off the record" understandably evokes feelings of a safe space, a cone of silence, a 'what happens in Vegas stays in Vegas' situation. Don't believe it. Nothing is ever off the record. Especially in this day and age where people have the ability to record your every move. From Presidents to John Q. Public, people continue to fall victim to things that were never supposed to be seen or heard.

Why? (That is not a rhetorical question!) These types of "gotcha" moments are well publicized and documented, so why do they keep happening? Do people think their position or influence somehow makes them immune to being recorded? Perhaps people think it could never happen to them. Maybe some people simply don't care.

Make a habit of guarding your lips, especially when you think no one is listening. It seems counterintuitive, but it will save you a world of heartache. None of us are perfect, and we all have opinions and prejudices that can produce some not-so-nice thoughts. But for goodness sake, don't say the quiet part out loud! There is too much of that going on already.

An entire school board displayed a terrible a lapse in judgment when they decided to have a conversation prior to the start of a Zoom meeting. Thinking they were not yet broadcasting to the public, the members of the Oakley Union Elementary School District Board in the San Francisco Bay Area began to deride the parents, at times using profanity (https://www.nbcnews.com/news/us-news/california-school-board-members-caught-disparaging-parents-accidental-zoom-broadcast-n1258351).

They discovered their mistake and switched the meeting to private, but it was too late. Despite apologies and excuses, a petition calling for the board to resign garnered more than 8,700 signatures. Each member of the board stepped down.

The mic isn't always a piece of equipment or a broadcast platform. It's also any place where your behavior is shown or where you make your opinion known. It still amazes me that people forget that social media platforms are the biggest tattle tales of them all. Are you one of those people? Don't be fooled by the false sense of power and popularity that ensnares so many people on social media.

Give careful thought to what you do and write. Every picture, video or post lives on in perpetuity. Nothing is ever truly deleted. There are companies whose sole purpose is to record and preserve online content, social media posts and websites. Even when you delete or unpublish the content, it still lives on...

One personal post you thought was a good idea at the time can cause you major professional problems down the road. A recent study by Career Builder found that 70% of employers use social media to screen candidates before hiring them, and 57% found content that caused them not to hire someone. You aren't necessarily safe once you're hired either; the same study revealed that 48% of employers use social media to check on their current employees and 34% have reprimanded or fired an employee due to the employee's social media activity.

When it comes to reputation, there is no separation between your personal life and your professional persona. One affects the other. You are, after all, the same person.

When you're tempted to say something you wouldn't say under different circumstances, just remember the tried and true advice you were given (hopefully) when you were young: if you don't have anything nice to say, don't say anything at all.

YOU CAN'T SHINE SH*T

An honest answer is like a kiss on the lips.

—Proverbs 24:26

A boss I had early in my career was fond of saying, "You can't shine sh*t!" It was her go-to phrase whenever someone asked her to make a bad situation look good. "You can't shine sh*t" was her way of saying that you can't disguise messy, smelly circumstances. No matter how you try to dress it up, a pile of poop is still a pile of poop.

This reminds me of a dog I once had named Trixie. She was a beautiful brindle boxer, mischievous and full of energy. As part of a routine check-up, Trixie's veterinarian asked me to bring in a sample of her poop.

Armed with an anti-odor pet waste bag, I took Trixie out for a walk. After the deed was done and bagged, I put the anti-odor bag inside of two regular pet waste bags, which were then sealed inside a ziplock freezer bag that was placed in a brown paper bag. I was ready for the 15 minute drive to the vet's office.

I got into the car carrying something that looked like lunch. A few minutes into the drive, a faint smell wafted up from the floor where I had placed the bag. There were five layers of defense between my nose and that poop, but with each passing minute the smell grew stronger. Even with all that camouflage, there was no mistaking what was in the bag.

It's the same way in life. Everything you do and say will eventually come to light. People can smell a cover up a mile away, so don't try to disguise it. Public relations is not a cure-all or a magic wand. You can't shine sh*t.

Inevitably, something will happen in your life or business that will be uncomfortable to talk about or will require immediate communication, whether or not you want to address the situation.

And, before you go there, 'no harm, no foul' is not a defensible position. Although you may be able to rectify an issue before the public gets wind of it, you still should be honest and inform your audiences about what transpired. People would rather hear the truth directly from you rather than learn about it on social media. With the former, you'll take one hit and bounce back. With the latter, you'll take a bigger hit and people will dig for more dirt because you have proven that you're not worthy of their trust.

So, what do you do when a crisis hits? Take hold of the situation. Get the facts. Understand what happened and decide what you're going to do to make the situation right. Now you're ready to step up to the mic. Pucker up and tell the truth.

Arm yourself with answers to the following questions:
- What happened?
- Why did this happen?
- Who is affected?
- What actions have been taken to rectify the situation?

- What steps are being taken to ensure this doesn't happen again?
- When will you give an update (if necessary)?

What seems hard in the beginning will pay big dividends in credibility. People respect honesty, even in the midst of anger and disappointment. Here's an example:

In December 2019, Zoom, a lesser-known business collaboration and videoconferencing company, averaged about 10 million users per day. By April 2020, the Zoom application was supporting 300 million people per day because of the increase in remote working and learning due to the coronavirus pandemic. The world (literally) was now counting on this company for connections to family, work, school, health care and a multitude of other critical ties.

The application's rapid expansion uncovered security flaws that caused a slew of problems for users, from surveillance and harassment to "zoom-bombing" attacks, where an uninvited guest hijacks the video call and takes control of the screen.

It would have been easy for Eric Yuan, the CEO of Zoom, to remain in the background while his chief information security officer or chief technology officer took the heat for the problems. It was, after all, a security and technology issue. The company could have made the deadly pandemic the center of attention or focused on the sudden explosion of users and what that could do to any software application.

Instead, Yuan gave the world a big 'kiss on the lips'. He addressed the situation in a truthful and timely manner; he didn't make excuses or throw anyone under the bus. Yuan outlined what happened, what was being done to correct it and pledged a higher level of accountability for himself and the company.

The immediate, straightforward and honest answers from the company gave businesses around the world confidence that the crisis was under control and the technical vulnerabilities would be fixed quickly. Because of Yuan's response, the incident was barely a blip on the radar; as of December 2020, the company's stock price had tripled, and Eric Yuan was named Time Magazine's Business Person of the Year 2020 (https://time.com/businessperson-of-the-year-2020-eric-yuan/). Smooches!

PART IV

CHILL DOWN

ARE WE THERE YET?

Seldom set foot in your neighbor's house
– too much of you, and he will hate you.

—Proverbs 25:17

Were you the kid in the back seat of the car who would ask incessantly, "Are we there yet?" during long drives? Fast-forward to the present. Are you still using that same annoying tactic to get a story published by your favorite media outlet?

At one large corporation I worked for, there was a school of thought that the best way to get a journalist to write about your news was to be overly persistent in your communication and follow up. It went something like this:

1. Send an email alerting the reporter about news coming up the following week.
2. Follow that with a media alert about the news happening soon.
3. Issue a press release via a newswire service.
4. Follow up with a phone call to ask if the news was seen.
5. Send the news again in an email and ask if they have any follow up questions.

6. Place a "when do you think you may write something about it" call if you don't see a story.

Are we there yet? Are we there yet? What about now? Are we there yet? Some reporters probably published a few lines about us just to stop the madness! There were far more who simply stopped responding to the constant drip of needless communication.

So, how do you repair the damage and go from being ghosted to getting back in a reporter's good graces? Here are four things that will help you build and grow a positive relationship with journalists: reconnaissance, reciprocity, respect and responsiveness.

Reconnaissance. Do a little research. Understand the topics and territory the reporter covers. This will keep you from sending press releases and pitches that are not relevant to what the reporter covers. Learn about the audience the reporter is writing for so you have a better sense of what news and angles the reporter will want to write about. Read the reporter's past articles or watch past interviews. Reporters want to know that you took the time to read what's been published. This will also give you ideas on what related story ideas you may want to pitch.

Reciprocity. Give before you get. Be of service before you ask for something. Make it a point to help the reporter without asking or expecting anything in return. Since you've done your reconnaissance, watch for trends and related news that would be of interest to the reporter and share a new discovery along with supporting statistics. Connect the reporter with a credible source who can speak on a developing news story from a perspective relevant to the reporter's audience.

Respect. Abide by the reporter's rules of engagement. Ask how the reporter likes to receive information. Remember the "how to get a reporter to write about you" process I mentioned previously? After I inquired about *how* and *when* the reporters wanted to receive information from the company, I received several different answers. It was more work for me to tailor the company's communications, but we received a sizable increase in coverage because of that change. Find out the reporter's deadline and stick to it. Timelines vary for each story, so always ask when the reporter needs to receive the requested information or conduct the interview.

Responsiveness. Assist expeditiously. Why spend all this time and effort building great relationships with reporters if you're not going to respond when they reach out to you? Return calls, emails, text messages, direct messages, etc., within 30 minutes if you can. You may not have the answer or the information requested right at that moment, but respond right away to let the reporter know you're working on it. There will be times when you are not able to help with a particular request, and that's okay. Let the reporter know that. Better yet - if possible - connect the reporter with another contact who can. While it would be great to be in every relevant story, the fact that you helped the reporter when there was nothing in it for your organization will practically guarantee that the reporter will keep you in mind for the next relevant story.

The digital world never sleeps, and it always needs to be fed. Follow the four "Rs" and you will build the trust and relationships with reporters that will lead to a better personal reputation and better corporate representation in the media.

CONTEMPLATION vs. SPECULATION

Do not boast about tomorrow, for you
do not know what a day may bring.

—Proverbs 27:1

Ever notice that forward looking statement at the end of a publicly-traded company's earnings announcement? It's written to remind investors that there are things out of the company's control that can change or prevent the company from achieving its stated goals.

A big part of public relations is managing expectations, and it starts with you. Be realistic about what you can accomplish, and take into consideration things that are beyond your control. Only God knows what will happen tomorrow.

Who could have predicted that 2020 would birth a pandemic, an economic crisis and worldwide demands for social justice unlike anything we've seen? In the midst of hardship, suffering and loss, there were still those whose arrogance compelled them to emphatically speculate there would be simplistic and imminent resolutions to all three. They were wrong.

Be measured in how you address what the future holds. Trouble comes when you get too boastful and promise outcomes based on your internal Magic 8-Ball. Peril awaits your reputation if you fail to deliver. Broken promises lead to broken trust. Without trust, your reputation is sunk. Negative comments and bad reviews live online in perpetuity.

Learn how to comfortably coexist with caveats. The word "caveat" has a negative connotation that's undeserved. Caveats simply bring balance to predictions. Balancing the intent of future accomplishments with a few caveats does not mean you lack conviction. It's simply a recognition that you can't control everything. (Use caveats responsibly; don't use them as a cover-up for being flaky, lazy or ill-prepared. Do the work!)

What you *can* control is what you do *before* you set expectations about what's ahead. It's easy to get excited about the new product or service you're about to announce - and that's ok! - but, your confidence in the future should be grounded in some serious contemplation.

Precede your course of action with sound research, a good dose of objectivity, and a thorough assessment of your capabilities and resources. What problem are you solving, and is it the *right* problem? Who are your ideal customers? What is your true cost of bringing that product or service to market? Have you developed a plan of action to deal with risks and disruptions? The list of things to contemplate is lengthy but necessary.

Even with perfect planning and the best of circumstances, stuff happens. Hence, the proverb! But, if you temper your forecast appropriately, you can weather the storm with far less backlash than if you simply boasted about what you planned to do.

When you're thrown that curve ball, remember you can't shine sh*t. (Yes, I shamelessly reminded you about a previous chapter in this book. The PR Proverb contained in it is *that* important!) Over-communicate about the situation, marrying your original plan and caveats with the adjusted course of action and expected outcome. If you have operated in good faith based on contemplation and hard work, people (more often than not) will understand and accept the shift, even though their frustration may be what is first expressed.

Invest in doing the best you can today, while planning as best you can for tomorrow. Only God knows what a day will bring, so leave the boasting to others.

FIGHT FIRE WITH GRACE

Do not answer a fool according to his folly,
or you yourself will be just like him.

—Proverbs 26:4

The older I get, the less patience I have for foolishness. It takes more effort to keep my facial expressions under control, and I have to pause a little longer before I respond verbally or in writing. If you sympathize - thank you. If you don't - keep living. It wasn't always this way for me; my tolerance level for nonsense was quite high earlier in my career. Too high, I discovered.

Have you ever worked with someone whose area of expertise had absolutely nothing to do with yours, but they felt the need to tell you how to do your job? I have. This co-worker took it upon himself to send emails to me frequently with suggestions on how I could do my job better. Whenever I would send out news or updates about public relations programs and results, I would see something from him in my inbox before the end of that day. Every. Single. Time.

I responded to him with all the professionalism I could muster, thinking that doing so would end the steady drip of unsolicited emails. It didn't. One day, he invited the business unit senior leaders into the conversation by copying them on his email. Game on. There was no way I was going to allow him to have the last word in front of this influential audience. So, back and forth the emails flew, neither one of us backing down and both of us landing not-so-subtle jabs cloaked in polite conversation.

I was writing yet another professionally worded but searing email when my office phone rang. I had been summoned to the principal's office. Feeling sheepish, I announced my arrival with a soft knock on the door frame. My boss looked up from a pile of paperwork but didn't speak. He just gave me that 'what-do-you-have-to-say-for-yourself?' look. I had been acting like I was 12-years-old, so I answered the unspoken question accordingly: "He started it."

In hindsight, the high level of foolishness I was tolerating was not his, it was my own. I let myself get dragged into an email tennis match of epic proportions because I was answering according to someone else's folly. There will be times when you have to and should respond to an issue, untruth or personal attack. When you do, remember words have the power to last far beyond the moment. Your responses should be grounded in two things: tact and timing.

Tact. To the casual observer, our center court display of email professionalism was just that, professional. But to those who knew how to read between the lines in each email, the barbed wire entwined with each pleasantry was razor sharp. Each nick and cut drew a little bead of blood that left a stain. While my comments may have been justified, I could have gone about making my point in a way that didn't diminish my light. I let the exchange get under my skin, and it cost me.

When foolishness comes your way, keep your focus on the issue at hand, and keep your emotions in check. Be direct, but season your responses with grace. Think more along the lines of killing with kindness rather than death by a thousand cuts! Having the last word isn't always a sign that you've won the argument. The opinion of those you serve is more important than the foolishness coming out of one person's mouth.

Timing. Some things may need to be addressed right away but many things don't. It's good to allow a cool-down period when possible. This is not just for the sake of the person you're setting straight, but for you as well! Give yourself the space and grace to gather your thoughts. Step back and reflect before answering.

Be mindful of the other person's environment, too. Pointing out a colleague's destructive behavior in front of that person's boss may be tempting, but listen to your better angels and have a private conversation first. Take away the stage, move the conversation off-line, smother the fire - anything that will minimize the issue going sideways or ballooning into something worse.

Fools will come and go. Focus your energy on what really matters and deal with foolishness on your own terms. There is nothing wrong with setting the record - or a person - straight. Pay attention to what you say, how say you say it and when you say it. Responding wisely will protect your reputation long after the fool is gone.

PART V

FUEL UP

WORKS AND WORDS

All hard work brings a profit, but mere
talk leads only to poverty.

—**Proverbs 14:23**

I love discovering the backstories of people I admire. It's wonderful to see people at the pinnacle of their careers, and it's fascinating to learn what it took for them to get there. We see the success, but we rarely see the sacrifice.

An abusive childhood, homeless and sleeping in a car for months, injustice and oppression, a hundred denials and closed doors, physical or mental health challenges; the list of what people overcame on their journeys is varied and truly amazing. The common thread? Hard work.

Read up on your favorite educator, actor, athlete, humanitarian, entrepreneur, missionary or musician. You may never grumble or complain about working hard - or anything else - ever again!

If you ask 10 people how they define hard work, chances are you will get several different answers. For me, it's less about volume and more about consistency. Sure, I've been in seasons of long hours and sleepless nights working on major projects, but seasons like those were not the ones that brought a profit. It was the sum of consistent hard work over time on small, seemingly insignificant projects that built trust and confidence with my audiences and influenced their point of view.

Are you consistent in the effort and importance you place on things you are asked to do? Do you take the same care with projects that are behind the scenes as those which are highly visible? Do you put in the same effort when you're a team member as you do when you're the team leader?

Be focused, diligent and dependable, even when you don't feel like it. Regardless of where you are and what you're doing, someone is always watching you to see if you are a good steward over what you have been given. Large or small, important or not, be consistent with your work ethic and profit will follow.

The profit isn't always financial. Profit can come in the form of credibility, trust, contracts, open doors, resources, access to the right people, opportunities, endorsements, etc. Profit that comes from hard work pays dividends now and in the future.

The flip side of this proverbial coin is mere talk. You've met them before - the Mere Talkers. They have style but no substance, always volunteer but never do anything, pose for the award picture but were MIA the entire project. I bet you're thinking of a particular person right now!

There's nothing wrong with being an effective orator. The ability to articulate a compelling vision and inspire people to action are important leadership skills. You may have people hanging on your every word, but your ensuing inaction will totally negate the value of those words. You must do more than just talk a good game to change perception or earn the stellar reputation you seek.

Years ago, I worked with a very compelling Mere Talker. He was smart and very knowledgeable about the industry and our competition, and could talk circles around anyone else in our business division. We both reported to the president of the division, but Mere Talker was the president's right-hand man. Rightfully so, until...

The business division president was called upon at the last minute to present information to the CEO and other senior leaders of the company. We were in the midst of a merger, and the other company's leadership would be participating via video conference. The president had one hour to pull everything together. The pressure was on.

I was in the president's office when he called in his right-hand man and asked him to prepare a portion of the presentation directly related to Mere Talker's responsibilities. "By the way," the president said, "I need it in 45 minutes." The look of panic gave away the answer before Mere Talker opened his mouth. He stammered and coughed and shifted his weight around before blurting out: "I can't. I can't do that. Sorry." He turned on his heel and left the room.

Our mouths dropped open. Literally. I was still in the *did that really just happen?* moment when I heard my name. I snapped out of my state of astonishment and looked at the president. I didn't like what I saw. I knew what that look meant. The president said that he was fully aware that the content was outside of my wheelhouse, but he needed my help.

He had other direct reports whose responsibilities more closely aligned with what needed to be done, so why did he ask me? He trusted me. I built a relationship of credibility and dependability with the president by delivering on every project and promise. He asked, "Will you pull together what

I need?" Outwardly, I replied, "I'll do my best." Inwardly, I screamed, *help me Jesus!*

Thankfully, God worked a miracle. I was able to pull together the necessary data and charts with two minutes to spare. The president combined our work and presented the information to the senior leadership of both companies to great reviews.

My hard work reaped profits of trust, credibility, promotion, the ear and favor of senior leaders, and other dividends that remain to this day. Mere Talker's poverty included the loss of respect from senior leaders and colleagues alike, as well as his position as the president's right-hand man. He was gone from the company soon thereafter, with a battered reputation in tow.

The next time you feel the need to talk your way into success, remember there will always be hard work and sacrifice required along the way. Are you willing and prepared to pay the price to get there?

As the saying goes: "Talk is cheap." I say, talk is never cheap when it's part of a package deal that includes integrity and a great work ethic. Work hard, follow up and follow through. Do what you say you're going to do, and be prepared to do what you profess to be able to do. If that's not possible, keep quiet.

THE BEST WAY TO BRAG

Let someone else praise you, and not your own
mouth; an outsider, and not your own lips.

—Proverbs 27:2

Finding that 'just right' volume of blowing your own horn is challenging. Too little, and it's easy to get overlooked or presumed to be less-than-leadership material. Too much, and you're pegged as an annoying blowhard or an insecure person who always needs attention and validation.

In situations when you need to self-advocate - a job interview, performance review, etc. - share information that's factual and contextual. Convey your accomplishments in terms of impact and effectiveness. The boast should be less about you and more about the outcome and team work that made it happen.

What about the rest of the time? Zip it. The best way to brag is to let others do the talking for you. Do your job well, and you'll find no shortage of people who will sing your praises.

The same is true for businesses. Conduct your business in such a way that makes it easy for your customers, vendors and the communities in which your business operates to say great things about your company and its products or services. The trust and credibility you build with your customers will deliver a higher return on investment than an advertising campaign any day of the week. Why? Because your prospective customers will believe someone else before they believe you.

A report by Kantar Media reveals that consumers trust advertising the least for information about brands and services (https://www.marketingcharts.com/cross-media-and-traditional/word-of-mouth-113276). That same report states that 93% of consumers turn to friends and family for information on brands and services. Review sites are the second-most trusted information source (91%).

The case for letting others praise you grows beyond the trust factor; according to a survey by BrightLocal, 94% of consumers say that positive reviews make them more likely to use a business (https://www.brightlocal.com/research/local-consumer-review-survey/?SSAID=314743&SSCID=81k5_8 qncq). Think about that. Because of another person's praise, what you offer will be trusted, sought out and purchased. Now, that's good business!

There are many effective ways to make your brand more visible and recognizable. You should use an appropriate mix of marketing tools to reach your goals. The purpose of this chapter (and the book!) is to help you lay a great foundation for building an excellent reputation. When customers, colleagues and even critics acknowledge a great product, service or program, it makes a much greater impact than any publicity you do on your own.

PLAY ABOVE YOUR WEIGHT CLASS

As iron sharpens iron, so one person sharpens another.

—Proverbs 27:17

For me, there's something comforting in knowing there are people who know a lot more than I do. A person who's been where I am on my life's journey and figured it out. A mentor I can learn from. An expert with answers. Not all folk feel that way.

There are those who'd rather remain a big fish in a small pond to preserve their status as the smartest person in the room. How can you expand your knowledge and sphere of influence if you only look to yourself for inspiration and answers? As the big fish, you teach others who have less experience, but who teaches you? If you're not learning, your lagging.

It can be intimidating to be in the same orbit as those who excel at their craft. Instead of jockeying to lead before you're ready, fall back and learn from that person instead. You'll expend less energy by drafting, and you will learn more, level up your expertise and be in a better position to lead others later.

That doesn't mean you don't have anything to bring to the table in the meantime! Your gifts and talents are unique to you. No matter how many people in the world share your occupation or skill set, no one can do the job like you can do it.

Start conversing with people who aren't your usual suspects. Expand your circle to the point where you are just a little bit uncomfortable in your new orbit. Hidden gems of wisdom can be found anywhere and at any time if you keep your eyes and ears open. You never know when a seemingly ordinary conversation can have significant impact down the road.

Little did I know that I was once on the road to being "restructured" out of a job, but God had other plans. In the immortal words of Adrian Monk (played by actor Tony Shalhoub in the hit TV series *Monk*), "Here's what happened..."

The company I worked for at the time was in the final phases of a merger with another industry powerhouse. For several days, the merger teams met off-site for high-level strategy sessions to determine every facet of the newly-formed entity.

One evening, our itinerary included a networking dinner away from the meeting venue. As I boarded one of the buses, I noticed a seat open near a group of work friends. I proceeded down the narrow aisle toward where they were seated. After a few strides, I saw an open seat next to an executive from my company - one of the best business and technical minds in the industry. I had two choices: smile, nod and keep walking to enjoy the ride with friends, or be a little bit uncomfortable and sit next to an executive I never had a chance to speak with outside of work. I sat down quickly before intimidation forced me to keep moving.

After the typical conversational pleasantries, I decided to ask one question: "So, how are your meetings going?" Then, I shut my mouth and just listened. It was one of the best decisions I've made in my entire career.

This executive was circumspect in his conversation, not revealing anything about the merger that was above my pay grade, but his insight into the industry, customers, competition and the market opportunity for our combined companies was invaluable. My knowledge about those subjects was equal to a big fish (me) in a small pond (the communications world I lived in). I quickly became a small fish with sharper fins and a greatly expanded perspective. Best. Bus. Ride. Ever.

The following morning, my first meeting of the day was replaced by an invitation from the other company's most senior communications executive to join her instead. It had already been determined that she would head up the new corporate communications function. The executive was leading a meeting to discuss advertising strategy for the launch of the new company. At the time, I was part of the corporate communications/public relations merger team; advertising was part of the marketing group's purview. The excitement of being a fly on the wall in another merger team's meeting faded the second I walked into the conference room.

The communications executive motioned for me to sit to her right; she said she "saved a seat for me." A senior product marketing executive from the other company entered shortly thereafter and sat to her left. Representatives from the advertising agency arrived as did others from the communication executive's team. I was the only person from my company in the room. *This is not good*, I thought. *Not good at all.*

I was silent for most of the meeting, as the topics discussed were mainly about specific product areas in which my company didn't compete. Then, the agency started a discussion about a main competitor, asking what about the merged company would keep the competitor "up at night."

The product marketing executive got right to his point: "They are afraid that we'll make a better product than they have." In a split second, the bus ride conversation came flooding back to me. The person from the agency replied, "That's it? This competitor's biggest worry is that your product will be better?" His answer: "Yes."

I took a deep breath and quietly disagreed: "It's more than that." Every head in the room swiveled in my direction.

I continued and, drawing on what I learned the night before, expanded the conversation from one product to the broader industry dynamic and what customer problems we had an opportunity to solve that would put the competitor in jeopardy. I folded in my area of expertise, bringing the conversation back to how we can better position ourselves not only in our advertising but in our overall communications and thought leadership efforts as well.

When I finished speaking, the communications executive (who had been staring in shock, alternating between me and the product marketing executive) asked him one question: "Is that right?" His answer: "Well...yes."

During the long flight home the next day, I decided to stand in the galley area for a few minutes to stretch my legs. One of our company's advertising managers happened to walk back to the galley and grew wide-eyed when he saw me.

"What did you DO yesterday?" My confused look prompted him to continue. "I was in a meeting yesterday, and we were talking about personnel for the merged corporation. The other company said they had to change their communications recommendations. They had written you off, thinking you were very nice but not much else, but whatever you said in a meeting caused them to go back and rethink everything!"

When I next saw the executive I shared the bus ride with, I told him about how he saved the day - and my job. Throughout his tenure at the company, he always took the time to share knowledge with me and my team. We all are better because of it.

Starting today, aim higher than your reach. Sharpen up by surrounding yourself with people who are smarter than you. Leave the kiddie pool behind and jump into the deep end. Give yourself room to grow. The world overflows with opportunity, and there is more than enough for everyone.

PART VI

PRE-FLIGHT CALIBRATION

GO! SET. READY?

It is not good to have zeal without knowledge,
nor to be hasty and miss the way.

—**Proverbs 19:2**

It was the first day of my first college public relations course. I made the mistake of listening to all the chatter before class started. Some of my classmates were boasting about their PR pedigree up to that point - prominent internships, high-profile events, notable connections, etc., - loud enough for everyone to hear.

At that moment, I made a decision to be the first to answer a question. I didn't have anything to brag about career-wise at that moment, but I knew what I knew and was going to make sure everyone else knew, too.

After the perfunctory review of the syllabus and setting students' expectations, the professor asked, "Who can tell me what the acronym FCC stands for?" My hand shot up before that last "C" left his mouth. I got the nod to answer, and I proudly did by blurting out: "Securities and Exchange Commission!"

Yikes! It was definitely a palm-to-the-forehead moment. I had just come from a finance class where we spent time talking about the SEC. My ears heard FCC but since my ego had taken over my brain, I thought I heard SEC. Talk about being hasty and missing the way!

It's understandable that every now and then you may get excited or caught up in the moment and blurt out something unintended. It's another thing entirely to intentionally fly by the seat of your pants instead of learning what you need to know.

One of the best things you can do for your reputation is acknowledge when you don't know something. It's not a sign of weakness, it's a sign of maturity and honesty. On camera or off, publicly and privately, it's ok to say, "That's a great question. I don't have the answer right now, but I will find out and follow up with you."

I love a saying I heard from leadership expert John Maxwell: "Before you attempt to *set* things right, make sure you *see* things right." There are always circumstances that you don't immediately see. What's the root of the problem are you trying to solve? Why do you think your perspective is the only perspective? Did you do due diligence justice?

Answer the tough questions before they're asked. There's nothing worse than great intentions that go horribly wrong because you didn't do your homework.

How many commercials have you seen where companies intended to convey messages that were powerful, unifying or funny but they ended up backfiring? You sat there and wondered, *What were they thinking?* or *Who in the world approved that?*

There will always be ads that miss the mark, some more spectacularly than others. In recent years, we witnessed Pepsi's Kendall Jenner Political Protest Campaign, which trivialized a worldwide social justice movement; the Dove body wash commercial where a chocolate-skinned woman morphed into a white woman after using the product; Bud Light's #UpForWhatever campaign, which promoted the tagline, 'The perfect beer for removing "no" from your vocabulary for the night'; and Hyundai's 'Our cars are so safe you can't even commit suicide in them' commercial that ran in the UK.

Whoever your target audience is, make sure you are talking to a representative sample of that audience about your big idea or game-changing plan before you put it in motion. When you get the right people in the room, listen with humility and an open mind. Your zeal without knowledge may be masquerading as a fantastic idea. You need someone to tell you the truth and burst your bubble before you go beyond the point of no return.

PRACTICE YOUR POKER FACE

Fools show their annoyance at once,
but the prudent overlook an insult.

—Proverbs 12:16

There are 42 individual muscles in the face. Scientists have determined that those muscles produce 21 categories of emotions (https://news.osu.edu/computer-maps-21-distinct-emotional-expressions--even-happily-disgusted/). Are your facial expressions in line with the words that are coming out of your mouth?

People can't read your thoughts, but they can understand the other signals you're communicating. Facial expressions and body language are dead giveaways to what's really on your mind. People are less likely to believe what you're saying if your body is speaking a different language.

Most of us had someone in our family who, with one look, "put the fear of God" in us when we were young. For me, it was my mom. For you, it may have been your Nana or Tia. I'm convinced they all share the same superpower.

My mom had several "looks," and I learned to distinguish between them very quickly. There was a difference, for instance, between the "What did you just say?" look and the "Don't you say another word" glare. I'll never forget the first time I experienced her "Just wait until we get home" stare from the choir stand when I was sitting in the church pews talking too much!

While my mom's expressions were definitely intentional, your unintended communication signals are more likely to cause your reputation harm.

It's easy to lull yourself into thinking your true thoughts are safe as long as you don't speak out loud what's going on inside your head. The audiences you engage with are smarter than that. People see more than you say.

Work at mastering your reactions. Our facial expressions can reveal how we really feel and what we're really thinking. I'm not suggesting that you should be disingenuous; when you remain calm and focused, you're better able to keep your verbal and non-verbal communication in sync. These mental muscles require constant exercise.

Start your workout by controlling your internal dialogue. During your next conversation, actively listen to the person you're speaking with instead of having an internal conversation about what you're going to say next or what you're going to eat for dinner. We can't stop thoughts from popping in our minds, but we can control how quickly we process or dismiss those thoughts.

Use your newfound internal dialogue discipline to help you guard against external landmines disguised as harmless conversation. Some statements are spoken specifically to get a rise out of you. Don't have a short fuse. Do your best to separate yourself from the insult or comment and stick to your message. If you take the bait, the conversation can go south very quickly.

Just ask Colonel Nathan R. Jessep. Played brilliantly by actor Jack Nicholson, Col. Jessep finds himself on the witness stand in a murder trial in the movie, *A Few Good Men* (Rob Reiner, Director. Columbia Pictures, 1992).

In every scene he appeared, the colonel's expressions oozed arrogance mixed with contempt, but more so when he faced the young JAG attorney who dared to summon him to court. The questioning that ensued led to one of the most infamous lines in pop culture and the most unforgettable scene in the movie.

Certain that intimidation and his position of power would bring his time on the stand to a quick end, Col. Jessep became more and more agitated as the lawyer called into question the colonel's actions and commands.

Col. Jessep gets caught up in his own arrogance and, just like that, the 'fool shows his annoyance' and ends up damning himself in the process. If he would have 'overlooked the insults', the outcome could have been much different.

If you haven't seen the movie, consider watching it. The courtroom scene with Col. Jessep is a 10-minute masterclass in how not to conduct yourself when the spotlight grows intense. It's also more proof that the Six Degrees of Kevin Bacon phenomenon is real.

DON'T BE STUPID

Whoever loves discipline loves knowledge,
but whoever hates correction is stupid.

—Proverbs 12:1

What does this have to do with your reputation? Everything. One of the best things you can do for yourself and your reputation is to remain teachable.

Correction can be constructive when given in love, but every now and then you're going to get called out by someone who intends to hurt you. How you view and respond during those times will either set you back or set you up for greater things.

One of my previous bosses was a constant critic. She felt she knew more than anyone about any subject, and she frequently expressed her dissatisfaction about those who fell short of her expectations. She found fault in everything everyone did, especially me. We had different skill sets, and she chose her strong suit, design, as a platform on which to stand and pass judgment.

A common opening statement when she reviewed my work was, "Let me tell you what I *don't* like..." She would then proceed to nit pick the assignment down to the smallest detail. Her motive was to tear down, but instead she built something she did not intend.

My eye for design and detail improved tremendously. I didn't realize it until I was working for another company, providing design guidance to my team on several marketing projects.

Those very projects won five international marketing awards for both content *and* design. The design awards may have been fewer in number had I not suffered - I mean, benefited - from her "feedback."

The point is, separate the criticism from the critic, then sift the criticism to find the hidden gems. Discard the rest. While my former boss' motives were not pure, she ended up helping more than hurting. She meant evil against me, but God meant it for good. (Genesis 50:20)

Be willing to listen, learn and course correct. Whether the motive for the correction is good or malicious, you'll be better off with the newfound knowledge.

Speaking of knowledge, resist the urge to dismiss or discount knowledge from those younger than you. The world changes rapidly; what we think we know about technology, trends, tribes and tactics will need to be updated within a few month's time.

Embrace the opportunity to learn from young people. The knowledge they possess, coupled with the wisdom and experience you wield, is an unbeatable combination.

PART VII

LAUNCH SEQUENCE IS A GO

BE AN ANSWER, NOT AN ARROW

Do not gloat when your enemy falls;
when they stumble, do not let your heart rejoice,
or the Lord will see and disapprove and turn
His wrath away from them.

—Proverbs 24:17-18

Let's be honest...little chuckle of glee may escape your lips when you hear of a competitor's mishap. Go no further. Kick a competitor when he's down and you may become ensnared in the same trap. As the saying goes: "There, but for the grace of God, go I."

While it may be tempting to join the chorus of those who are ridiculing the competitor, step back instead. Hold up a mirror; are you also vulnerable to the same problem, trouble or crisis? Don't be so quick to judge or point out the vulnerabilities of others. It is an open invitation for people to start digging in your backyard.

This happens on social media every hour, it seems. A person will post something ridiculing another individual or company, thinking that by doing so it will cause embarrassment or harm. But, quicker than you can swipe, the person who pointed the finger is now on blast because of something they said or did that was just as bad - or worse.

Truthfully, none of us can afford to point out someone else's shortcomings. We've all made mistakes. That's not to say that you should never address a serious issue or wrongdoing. The point here is to come at it from a position of offering a solution, not condemnation.

Be an answer, not an arrow.

Know your strong suit so you will be prepared to step into an opening when one presents itself. For instance, if one of your competitors lands in the spotlight because of an employee's horrendous customer service, but you have an incredible customer service training program as part of your new hire onboarding process, speak up!

Quickly but thoroughly prepare messaging and tailor the content for your various communications channels. Don't dog-pile on the competitor; talk about the broader issue and offer helpful advice. Make this a learning moment.

You can do this in an infinite number of ways: start a customer appreciation campaign on social media featuring videos of happy customers, write an op-ed piece on the dying art of customer service, place a byline article in an industry trade publication about your customer service training and the measurable difference it's made, pitch stories about employees who go above and beyond in serving customers, or post a blog about the top 10 ways to delight customers.

So, what's your company's (or your) superpower? You don't have to wait until something hits the fan and a competitor goes down for the count. Start building content now. It should be part of your ongoing thought leadership and reputation management efforts.

Being an answer is good not only for industry-wide issues but for your personal reputation as well. When the most difficult, unlikable person in your department slips up and heads are about to roll, be the first to step up with a way to rectify the situation. Problem solvers are always held in high esteem.

When something goes sideways, many people choose to stand at a safe distance while keeping track of what happened, who did it and the damage that was done, and then take bets on the severity of the consequences. While that may be entertaining, it's counterproductive. There will be plenty of time to analyze what went wrong later.

Be the answer the situation needs right now. That's what people will remember.

LIFT AS YOU CLIMB

A generous person will prosper; whoever refreshes others will be refreshed.

—Proverbs 11:25

Growing up, my brothers and I spent most summers in Texas where our mom was born and our grandparents lived. That was the only time we would get to go crabbing. When those traps came out, we knew that grandma's gumbo wasn't far behind! One thing that always fascinated me was how the crabs behaved once they were moved from the traps into the big, white buckets that were used to transport them home.

During my first crabbing trip, I became alarmed when I noticed a crab trying to climb out of the bucket. "Mom!" I yelled, "Where is the lid for the bucket? The crabs are trying to climb out!" Busy with another trap, my mom looked up and smiled. "Don't worry, the other crabs will take care of it." Sure enough, I looked back at the bucket and saw the other crabs pulling down the fleeing crab.

Crab mentality. It's a dangerous frame of mind. The only perspective is, "If I can't have it, neither can you." Anyone who cleaves to this view will hold you back or hold you down.

A person with crab mentality fails to realize that by pulling others down, they doom themselves to a bottom-of-the-bucket existence. If no one makes it to the top, who is going to reach back and lift up the next person?

Imagine if public relations professionals suffered from crab mentality. We're supposed to lift people (or organizations) up not prevent them from reaching higher heights. Being successful in the field of public relations takes education, training, experience and a lot of wisdom, but if you don't like to see other people succeed, you're in the wrong business!

Looking out for the needs of others requires a generous spirit. Make it a habit to be generous and refresh others, especially those who are not in a position to reciprocate.

Before you default to thinking that giving money is the only way to be generous (although some do need that type of blessing), remember that generosity takes on many forms. You can share your time, talent, resources, encouragement or just be nice. The good you do can come back to refresh you in a way that is completely unrelated to the kindness you showed.

One particular story, shared by Gospel music legend, producer and Grammy Award-winning artist Fred Hammond during a Sunday church service at The Potter's House, is an amazing example of this principle.

After his ground-breaking Gospel group *Commissioned* disbanded, Hammond launched out as an independent artist. He handled everything personally, including booking gigs. That's how his contact information ended up in the hands of two 17-year-olds who called Hammond's phone number at 2:00am, just hoping to hear an answering machine recording of the voice of someone they admired. Hammond picked up the phone.

The two teens apologized profusely, thinking they were about to get the tongue lashing of their lifetimes. Instead, Hammond took the time to talk with the two young men, asking them about school and their grades, thanking them for listening to his music, and encouraging them to keep God first. The two promised that they would.

More than two decades later, Hammond was dealing with knee pain that was at times excruciating. During a video shoot in Washington, D.C., an onlooker noticed that Hammond was limping around on the set. Concerned, the man approached the music icon and introduced himself. He was one of the teens who called Hammond at 2:00am all those years ago. As they talked about the condition of Hammond's knees, the man paused to call his childhood friend who was now a leading orthopedic surgeon in Texas. You see where this is going, right?

The two friends shared how much it meant to them that Hammond had been so nice on the phone, talking with them and encouraging them. They wanted to repay Hammond's kindness. The doctor not only performed the much needed double-knee replacement surgery on Hammond, but he significantly reduced the cost of the surgery and hospital stay as well. "...He who refreshes others will himself be refreshed."

It's easy to dismiss small acts of kindness as unimportant. But it's the small things - a helping hand, a second chance, a kind word to strangers at two o'clock in the morning - that take us farther faster than the big battles and victories.

Mikki Taylor, editor-at-large for Essence Magazine, author, motivational speaker and entrepreneur, said something during a conference I attended that stuck with me: "Create your empire, and bless others along the way." Help someone reach their next level. Trust me, doing so will not hinder your upward progress.

If you ever find yourself looking up from the bottom of the bucket at someone who is climbing and clawing their way to the top, be the person who gives them the lift they need to make it over the edge. You'll receive that kindness back in spades as you climb your way to the top.

READY TO LAUNCH

Commit to the Lord whatever you do,
and He will establish your plans.

—**Proverbs 16:3**

Our journey began by acknowledging God and trusting Him to give us wisdom and to make our paths straight. We now come full circle to commit our plans to Him as we stand on the launch pad to an exceptional reputation.

This will be a process. Mastering every PR Proverb at once is an admirable goal, but not necessary; pick an area to start with and grow from there. Each day will bring a new opportunity to shift your thinking. Use each circumstance to develop a mindset of being better and doing better.

As you start walking your talk and abiding by what you've learned in this book, you will notice a change in not only yourself, but in those around you. Some people will level up while others will fall away the higher you ascend. That's ok. Everyone can't go where you're headed. Surround yourself with people who exemplify an excellent character or, at the very least, have a kinship with you when it comes to building a better reputation.

Authenticity is better than perfection. Keep this in mind as you embark on your journey. Be you, do you and stay true to who you are. Your starting point may not be ideal, but don't put off taking action until everything is perfectly aligned. Write down your vision, and create a plan of action. Keep track of milestones and accomplishments, making adjustments as you go.

Now that you have created a launch pad for an exceptional personal and professional reputation, where will you go? What will you do? What results are you seeking?

Do you need to repair a damaged reputation? Breathe new life into a mature brand or build a new one? Launch a new product or service? Break through the market noise? Increase demand for your service or products? The road you choose will be easier because you have created the right atmosphere for success by building an exceptional reputation.

If you need a high-level framework to get you started, fear not! You didn't come this far just to be stranded on the launch pad with no fuel for a successful launch. The following seven steps will help you plan for and stay on course during your journey.

1. **Audience.** Know your publics. Who are you trying to reach? Which audiences are key to your success? Which influencers affect your audiences' perceptions and behaviors?

2. **Assess.** Get an objective and accurate view of the current perception of you or your business among your key audiences. If you have the resources to do so, hire a firm to conduct a brand assessment. You can also do this yourself by holding focus group sessions.

3. **Adjust.** Once you receive the assessment results or focus group feedback, be prepared to make

adjustments in your actions or approaches to rectify unfavorable perceptions. Adjust your expectations that a few ads, social media posts or press releases will cure everything. Put in the work.

4. **Aim.** None of this shoot, ready, aim business! Aim first. What's your target? What are you trying to accomplish and by when? Develop your plan. Determine your goals, strategy for reaching them and the actions you'll take to get there.

5. **Actualize.** Get to it! Execute your plan, but stay flexible to adapt to new challenges and opportunities. If public relations is new to you, don't bite off more than you can chew. It's better to do a few things well than many things poorly. You want to show your audiences consistency and progress.

6. **Achieve.** How will you know when you achieved your goals? What will success look like? Perception change cannot be measured in interviews, clicks or website visits. Engage your audiences in two-way communication on multiple levels so you can accurately identify trends and shifts in perception.

7. **Analyze** What did you accomplish? Evaluate which strategies were effective. Fine-tune aspects of the plan that need to be more impactful. Time to re-assess to see how the perception needle has moved.

Take time to celebrate what you accomplish along the way, whether it's a small change or a major breakthrough. Before moving on to your next conquest, make sure you keep the promises and commitments you made to the audiences that now perceive you in a new, better light. An exceptional reputation is not a 'one and done' endeavor. It's a lifetime commitment and a legacy that will live on long after you're gone. So, be honest. Crave knowledge. Speak with substance. Listen more. Do right by others. Hold your relationships in the highest esteem.

Prepare for ignition and launch with confidence, knowing there will always be a proverb you can learn from.

Three, two, one...lift off!

ACKNOWLEDGMENTS

Do not withhold good from those who deserve it,
when it is in your power to act.

—Proverbs 3:27

Thank you Jesus - the Lord of my life, the redeemer of my soul, my best friend and my everything - for all you poured into me so I could pour out to others. Mom, thank you for modeling what an excellent reputation looks like and lives like. To my daughter, Natasha, you make me a better person. I am blessed because you are in my life.

I'm grateful for the executives, managers, mentors and colleagues who were kind enough to share a bit of wisdom with me; I'll continue to pay it forward. Thank you to all who inspired me to keep moving, keep striving, keep writing. You knew one day the momentum would carry me beyond gravity's reach. To God be the glory!

ABOUT THE AUTHOR

Whoever gives heed to instruction prospers,
and blessed is the one who trusts in the Lord.

—Proverbs 16:20

Glynnis Woolridge is the CEO of Salt & Light Enterprises, LLC. An award-winning public relations strategist, communicator, and brand and reputation management expert, she advises individuals and organizations on how to create, build, leverage and protect the value of their brands. Visit www.glynniswoolridge.com.

www.ingramcontent.com/pod-product-compliance
Lightning Source LLC
Chambersburg PA
CBHW071456210326
41597CB00018B/2573